Letters to Another Life

Nicholas McDaniel

Table of Contents

Dedication – 4

Scarlett Daniels - 6

From the Beginning – 7

13 Years Left – 28

You are Inconceivably Evil – 75

5 Years Left – 90

Dying of the light – 105

Biography - 133

Dedication

To all the people who have supported me along in writing this book, thank you. None of this would have been possible without you. You are the reason I write, and I continue writing. I never thought I'd write again after *helios and his moon*, but I decided to give it another shot. The amount of support and love I've gotten during the writing process of this book has been incomprehensible. Nothing could've prepared me for the outreach I have had on people's lives. My passion has reached millions, and I am blessed I have a voice that likes to be heard. Take this time, before you begin reading, to think of your voice. Think of the things you'd like to say. Think of the life you have yet to live. Where will you be in a year from now? Two?

I never thought my passion would turn into a career. I never thought my voice would be so heard.

I dedicate this book to the unheard voices. To me, you've made my life whole.

Dedication

Special thanks to:

vi/stevelcys
Joslyn Aguilar
Samantha Miller
Vanessa Sierra
katie/mushroomvrcp
Iota Delta
Cheyenne
Jesse McEntire
Justin Parks
Hayden Roeder
Chelsea/koneneon
Joshua Saavedra
Faith
Caeley Diane
Jade S.
Talia Thompson
Elias Gennaoui
Ryan Konrad
Shelby Humphreys

Demetri Gonzalez
Aaron Vasquez
Rudy Ponce
Drew Jedi Ruiz
Eric Esquibel
Lauren Cassidy
Michael Oceguera
Myrna Abarca
Kayla Lopez
Kenny Lorenzana
Jamal Hanaif
Raul Ramirez
Cal & Amanda
Hannah Rath
Tyler
Lyssa
Mom & Dad
Mark McDaniel Jr.
Ryan Gosling

Scarlett Daniels

Hello,

My name is Scarlett Daniels, I am 23 years old, and I am dying. In fact, if you are reading this, I am dead. I was diagnosed with lung cancer 4 years before my demise and chose to fight it out. I was always seen as a fighter by my friends and family. I'd like to think cancer didn't beat me, however. I'd like to think it was a tie. Better record for me, haha. The cancer started spreading, breathing became hard, and I just wanted to live the rest of my life in peace.

All I want is to live again. My life was stripped from me at such a young age, and I didn't even get to live. This letter, alongside all my other letters, are meant to be published for the world to see. I want my future life to see who I was, and perhaps even remember me. I want to continue where I left off in the next life. I have too many unspoken words.

These are events from my life through my eyes. The eyes of a dying girl. Through my words, you will know my struggle. You will know my life. You will know me. Please, remember me.

Until next time,
S.D.

From the beginning.

To my beautiful daughter,

It is my blessing to have you as my daughter. You have been in my lil tummy for the past 8 months, and you're almost out!! You are a fighter, let me tell you. You kick and kick for what seems like hours at a time. I cannot wait to be your mother. I am so giddy every single day with your dad. We are going to give you such a beautiful life.

To my future Scarlett, you will be my daughter for as long as we shall live. You will be me, and I will be you. You will be the best and worst of me, and I can do nothing but give you the love I never had as a child. I will support you through anything in life, and we will be best friends. We will be that cute little mother and daughter duo.

There is nothing in life more rewarding than our life spent together. You are my most prized possession. We will meet each other soon, and I will give you this letter when it is time.

I love you so much, Scarlett Daniels.

Sincerely,
Mommy.

Happy mothers
day mommy!

I Love
you
so much

—Scarlett

Hi mommy im really mad at you becaes
youre making me rite evry thing down
becaues you want to keep them for later. im
a big girl mommy i am in second grade I
dont' like riting. I dont' know why you were
crying yesterday at the docter. even I wasnt
scared of the docter!!!! im also mad at you
since you said we have to go back next
week.

also can we get a cat mommy.

I loveeeee youuuuuuuuuu

scarlett

June 17, 2007

I am so sorry, my sweetpea.

All I wanted to do was protect you and I just couldn't. You are too young to go through this.

Fuck that.

There is no part of my life that could've prepared me for this.

I am so sorry.

I feel like this is my fault.

The doctors told me they suspected it, but I couldn't believe them.

I love you so much

mommy take me to the docter again and she gav me shots. it hurt me rely bad. she gav me pictures also. she put me in a big giant masheen and it was so cool!

mommy was sad.

mommy also said we can get a cat!!!!!!

i love you so much mommy!!!

scarlett

the
docter
masheen

mommy got a kitty!!!!!!!
i am soooooo xsited.
mommy is still relly sad tho. i dont' no why.

i also dont' no where daddy is.

he dusnt come to the docters with me or
mommy.

he also dusnt come to my home any mor.

and that is relly sad.

scarlett

October 5, 2007

Me and Terry divorced. I think Scarlett
knows. He doesn't come around anymore; I
don't think he wants anything to do with us.

I miss him.

I got Scarlett a cat. It's the least I could have
done.

Scarlett has done well in her journal so far.
She hasn't written in a while, ever since the
treatment started getting worse.

My poor girl lost her hair.

She had to miss the first couple months of
3rd grade, and the boys have been really
mean to her.

Besides Leo. He's a nice kid.

i came back to thurd graed. i had to come late becaus of me being sick.

the uther kids bully me becaus I have no hair.

and it makes me really sad.

leo is really nice to me tho.

oh yeah, leo is my frend.

scarlett

mommy dosnt smile with me any more.

she thinks i dont' know what cancer is.

i saw it on a comershal.

im a big girl mommy,

dont' lie to me.

scarlett

December 24th, 2007

Tomorrow is Christmas! Better yet, tomorrow is my beautiful baby's birthday. Scarlett has told me she knows what cancer is, so I guess there's no more putting up a front.

The doctor said it's looking good, which is such good news.

She has also told me about her little crush now, Leo. She refuses to write about him, but I keep trying to push that on her.

She's a fighter, isn't she?

She's definitely my girl.

mommy got me hair for xmas.

she made it blond which is relly cool cus
that is like my hair.

but longer.

i put it on at school and no one makes fun of
me any more.

I think kids forgot about it.

leo also called me pretty with hair.

am i only pretty with hair.

scarlett

I sat next to leo today at lunch.

and yesterday, too.

He asked if I like to play gamez and I said yes. He wants to play with me.

That maed me very happy because I think I like leo.

also my frend monica invited me to her hous and it was super cool.

It was relly big. and her mom is nice.

but I think her mom made fun of me. I think I listen to her talk about my hair.

scarlett

me and monica went to the store today to get candy and I saw my dad their.

I got super duper happy when I saw my dad but he didnt' see me. that made me sad.

I think he saw me achtualy. he saw me and looked away fast.

I hope he is happy where ever he is.

monica got chips and I got candy.

not spicy chips tho.

those hurt me too.

scarlett

June 15, 2009

Scarlett took a break from writing for a while, and so did I. We've been spending a lot of time together in the past year or so. This is exactly what we've both needed. Her hair grew back, so no need for a wig anymore.

Thank God, she hated it. It made her sweaty.

She's also been a lot more social in school, Mr. Jacobs even said she talks a lot, which I can't really be mad about. Leo comes over a lot, and so does Monica. Those are two of her best friends, and she keeps it obvious that she likes Leo.

I don't think she'll stop liking Leo. I think he likes her back.

My beautiful girl is going to start 5th grade soon. I am more excited than her, to be honest.

I started the fifth grade today!! I am so excited. I got to pick my seats and monica is in the class so we are sitting next to each other. Leo isn't in the class so I am sad.

My teacher is really old and kind of scary haha. Luis and Teresa are also in this class so im excited because I want to be their friends.

I also think I know what I want to do when I am older.

I want to be a writer.

I have a presentation today about your favorite animal. I love monkeys. theyre so cool.

and I think leo knew this, because he got me a monkey stuffed animal and it was soooooooooo cute. I got so excited when I saw it.

when I presented, I got a lot of claps at the end. everyone loved my presentation!! the teacher called me a natural so I was happy.

my mom got me ice cream after school.

I got vanilla.

no toppings.

Scarlett

Its December 18 today and it's our last day of school before xmas break. It's also a week before my bday!! I am so excited I am finally going to be 10 years old.

Leo got me a necklace! I also gave him a hug and everyone was watching. Everyone laughed and I got super embarrassed. But I think he liked the hug.

And I think he likes me, too.

Monica gave me a letter and she was telling me how she loves me! She is my best friend omg.

I think I want to tell leo I like him.

Scarlett

December 25, 2009

Scarlett turned 10 today!! I can't believe my beautiful, strong girl is the girl she is today. She's come so far, and she has made me the happiest lady in the world.

All I need is her by my side. It's just me and her at the house, and I cannot help but see myself in her. She laughs at everything I laugh at. She cries at everything I cry at.

She told me she wants to be a writer. There's not much money in that field, haha, but I have all my faith in her. She's going to change this world and the next, I just know it.

Leo also got her a necklace. That boy is in love, let me tell you.

13 years left.

Guess what??

Mommy got me a phone!! Finally!!

I am so happy, it took me soooo long to convince her. She kept saying no and no and no but for xmas, she got me one. She was just tricking me. Silly mom.

She told me to not give my phone number to boys though. Because boys can be mean.

Not Leo though, he's never mean to me.

But I don't want to get it taken away, so I'll give it to Monica first.

Two best friends!

Scarlett

"Hi scarlett!!! It's monica this is my phone."
2:51 pm

"OMG!! Heyyyyy girl. It's scarlett. I told
you mommy would get me one for xmas!"
3:27 pm

"Haha. Don't call her mommy. That's for
little girls. We're big now!!"
3:30 pm

"Ok"
3:55 pm

"Did you see johnny today??"
3:56 pm

"Yes what about it?"
4:21 pm

"He looked cute right?"
4:22 pm

"Idk I wasn't looking a lot"
4:43 pm

"Do you still like Leo?"
4:44 pm

"Hahaha girl you know I like him still"
5:25 pm

"Yeah, I know."
"You tell me a lot"
5:26 pm

I want to leave fifth grade now. I saw leo
talking to another girl and it just makes me
so sad.

I want to tell my mommy but shes just going
to tell me to suck it up. That's inapropriete.

Mommy has been mean to me so I talk to
monica more.

I don't know why.

I can listen to music now and it's really cool.

Sometimes I like listening in the rain. Under
the sheets. Sometimes I turn the light off.
And I really like that.

And I also think monica is jealous that she
doesn't like someone like I do.

Scarlett

Mommy wants me to start walking to school
instead of her driving me. It's not far but
that is scary.

I also want to get over leo but I cant. I also
didn't tell mommy. I wish she listened to me
like before. maybe its because im older now.
Maybe its because she wants another kid.
But daddy left so she cant.

I wonder if itll ever be like it was before.
I wonder if she'll listen to me like she did.

i wonder how itll be when im older

I found Scarlett's journal. I knew all about her little friends and crush, but why does she feel like she can't talk to me anymore? I'm always there for that little shit. I buy her shit and I make sure she's always spoiled.

I know she misses her dad but fucking christ im here too.

She thinks she's such a big girl now which is why I'm making her walk to school now. It's a few blocks north. It's not as big of a deal as she's making it.

Maybe this is just how raising girls can be.

I wonder how mommy would have been if daddy never left.

maybe she would have taken care of me more.

maybe she would have cared more.

I wonder why Monica is mad at me all the time. Girls just get jealous with each other.

Im jealous of the girl Leo talks to.

Scarlett

I just started sixth grade today!! Moved to a new school, and not everyone moved with me which is sad. Monica and Leo are still with me so that's cool.

I think leo broke up with his girlfriend which is nice because now I can be his girlfriend.

I think Monica wants to be with leo still. She gets mad every time I talk about him.

I also don't like how I have to move to different classes now. I have so many teachers. I don't have leo for any classes either.

I'll see how this year goes.

Scarlett

I have so much homework, and school is so annoying. There are so many new people and it's kinda scary. Im meeting all these new people and I am just kinda scared to be judged.

I have my headphones on a lot. My teachers get mad at me though, so I put them on after class.

I walk home now too. It's relaxing. I listen to music on the way home. I walk a lot more too.

I guess my mom stopped caring in that way.

Scarlett

Writing in this journal is so embarrassing. Little girls do this, and I'm not little anymore. I need to grow up. I want to grow up. I want Leo to notice me and I don't think he does.

I watch him but im too scared to say anything. People don't wonder about me anymore either.

Im scared no one cares like they used to.

Scarlett

Scarlett threw her diary away again.

I had to dig through the trash to get it. She's difficult to work with these days. It's hard to live with just her. I picked up more hours at work just so I can be away a little more. I love that girl to death, but she needs to learn how to be more independent. She's just a little heartbroken that her little boyfriend doesn't talk to her anymore. We'll see how she gets.

I love my daughter, don't get me wrong.

I just wonder why she needs me so much.

Hey, Diary (?)

Yup, it's me again. I took a break. A long one, at that. I forgot I even had this thing, it's pretty funny to look at, haha.

Before I continue with normal entries, let me update a little.

I'm a freshman in high school now. Being a big girl isn't as fun as it seems. Leo talks to me here and there, but he's a popular guy and I'm not really in that group.

He joined football. I joined the poetry and writing club.

Monica stayed with me. I noticed the less I talk about Leo, the more she talks to me, so I've just mentioned him less and less.

I don't have a relationship with mom anymore. She leaves early and comes back late. It hurts, but I have my own stuff to take care of.

I still want to be a writer when I grow up, so I intend to keep this diary as "practice", I guess.

I'll still treat this as a normal diary, but I'll add a few things to it I suppose.

High school is scary. A lot of these guys are scary. Girls are even meaner than before. I also saw my first fight, which was kind of exciting.

I hate being a wallflower. I hate being a nobody.

I hate that people don't ask about me anymore.

Anyways,

I'll update whenever I can.

Scarlett

Hey Diary,

I found new friends! They were all in my biology class, and we happened to be in the same group. They all went to middle school together, and they want to hang out with me.

It's two guys and two girls, with me included. It's a pretty good balance, I think at least.

The two guys are Jason and Justin, which is a pretty easy duo to remember. The girl is Violet, which is such a pretty name.

I can't wait to hang out with them tomorrow, we're supposed to go to Jason's house after school for a bit.

Seeya later!

Scarlett

"OMG MONICA"
3:34 pm

"YES?"
3:35 pm

"I think they want to smoke weed right
now"
3:38 pm

"Girl what the fuck??"
"What are you gonna do?"
3:38 pm

"Maybe I'll try a little, my mom won't be
home until late anyways."
3:42 pm

"Monica?"
3:50 pm

"MONICA I just tried some"
3:52 pm

"How do you feel?"
3:53 pm

"Holy shit"
4:05 pm

Hey Diary,

I tried weed yesterday. Jason showed me a "joint" and asked if I wanted to try it. I said no, but everyone else had some.

They called me a bitch for not wanting to smoke, so I did. I could not stop coughing.

I felt really good. I was super high. I wanted to eat everything in my sight haha.

I walked home and listened to music. It was pretty dark. I almost started crying.

Note to self: Don't listen to music while being high.

I don't want this to be a regular thing though. I got pretty paranoid.

Scarlett

Hey Diary,

It's my birthday.

Big 15!

No one told me happy birthday besides Monica. Mom got presents but it was for Christmas. I think she might've forgotten it's actually my birthday today too.

I don't even feel like I have a mom right now. I don't even feel like I have a solid friend group.

Yes, Jason, Justin, and Violet are cool, but they're new, so only time will tell if they're the right group for me.

I haven't even thought about Leo.

Scarlett

Hey Diary,

Welp. This is quite the start to an entry.

Leo said hi to me today. And without sounding too desperate, it meant a lot.

He hasn't acknowledged my existence since the beginning of the school year, so I don't know why he chose to say hi to me today of all days.

He looked damn good though, I'll say that much.

Maybe I'm not over him. Maybe I never will be over him.

Jason and I went to the park after school today. He wanted to smoke more but I decided not to. I think Jason likes me.

He's a pretty sweet guy, but I just can't see myself with him. I told this to Monica, and I don't think she's as jealous. She doesn't seem threatened by Jason as she is by Leo, and I really don't know what that's about.

Scarlett

until I decide to breathe
you'll keep treating me like this
you'll stick me in your bag
and pull me out only when you need it
a bag of tricks
like I'm supposed to solve your problems

until I decide to breathe
you'll take me for granted
you'll come home to me
because it's easy for you
and hard for me to leave
we used to be a team

once I decided to breathe
I was the bad guy
your life was hell
and it was all my fault
you made me believe
a simple breath
of retaliation
was an act of violence

if I looked better
acted better
would you have loved me
would you have let me breathe

I didn't think
me signing my life away
to be yours
was an act of defiance
so why was I treated
like it was

what if I had changed everything
and let you have your ways
I loved you and I am sorry
what if I was better
maybe then
you would've let me breathe.

scarlett

Hey Diary,

How was that?

Was that a good poem?

For poetry club, we had to write one poem about any topic, so I did that. It was actually my first "real" poem I've written, and I decided to make it free verse.

Monica really liked it. Jason really liked it. Justin and Violet don't really like poetry, so I didn't bother showing them.

At times, I wish I could show Leo.

I feel like I'm getting over him though. Finally.

                                        Scarlett

Hey diary,

It was the last day of school today. End of freshman year, I guess. I ended with 2 A's and 4 B's. Not terrible, I can't be mad at that.

Leo said bye to me today. Ugh. I don't know why he constantly plays these games with me. Monica saw it and just scoffed, as did I.

Jason also told me he liked me today, and I didn't really know what to say. I kinda froze in shock, but I let him know that we'll always be friends. He didn't like that response, but what do I really owe him?

Justin and Violet called me their best friends. That really warmed my heart. I don't hang with them much, so hearing that was really nice.

Until next time,

Scarlett

What the fuck?

Leo texted me.

"Hey, Scarlett.
I know we don't talk like we used to, and I want to change that. We were always such close friends through school, and I really became distant. Basically, what I want to say is sorry. I want to keep talking to you, and I don't want our friendship to get as distant as it once was."
3:01 am

"Oh?"
10:09 am

"Haha, I know it was a late text so sorry about that."
11:54 am

"No no no don't worry about it, it just caught me off guard."
"We should talk more"
11:56 am

Hey Diary,

Me and Leo have been talking all summer. Every. Single. Day. It's heaven on earth LMAO.

I don't know, I think he really does like me back. We always talk about going to places together, knowing damn well neither of us can. I ask Monica for ideas of how I should impress him or give gifts to him, and she always just shoots it down.

It genuinely upsets me that she can't just be happy for me. I want to talk to her about it.

Scarlett

"Monica can we talk"
4:07 pm

"Yes what's up?"
4:08 pm

"Do you like Leo?"
4:11 pm

"No I don't scarlett."
4:12 pm

"Then why the fuck can't you be happy for me?"
"You know how long I've liked him, and you just never seem to support me with it"
4:20 pm

"I know, im sorry."
"I just feel like you deserve better"
4:21 pm

"What do you mean?"
4:28 pm

"He barely talks to you."
4:29 pm

"We talk every day, what do you mean?"
4:31 pm

"No, I know that, I'm saying he doesn't
TALK to you."
4:32 pm

"Can you clarify?"
4:36 pm

"He doesn't try to understand you scarlett.
He's too surface-level with you. He doesn't
try to show you his actual character. He
doesn't talk to you the way I do."
4:38 pm

"Okay"
4:44 pm

Hey Diary,

I don't think Monica wants to talk to me anymore.

After our argument (if you can even call it that) we haven't said anything to each other. She doesn't seem to understand what I feel for Leo, or what Leo feels for me.

Justin, Jason, and Violet want to hang out with me soon.

Maybe they'll come pick me up here, Justin has a car. Jealous.

I hope Monica doesn't get too upset with me, I really do like spending time with her.

Scarlett

Hey Diary,

I smoked weed again.

It was better this time, I didn't feel as paranoid. I feel a little guilty, but not too bad.

I was gonna invite Leo, but I didn't want to overstep with this friend group.

I also am still scared about Leo and what Monica said. Does he really not care about me? Is he just bored?

No, we're different than that. I just gotta get to the bottom of it.

Also weed is the first thing in a while that makes me feel this alive.

Scarlett

Hey Diary,

It was the first day of 10th grade. I saw Leo, and we hugged. It was so serene. So nice. It was a quick one, at that, but it felt so needed and necessary. It felt as if, for once, I finally felt wanted in my life.

Not only did I feel wanted- I felt alone. I finally felt alone in this world with the one person I wanted to be with. Like nothing else mattered, like nothing else was real. It was me and him in a maze to find each other, and we did. I saw myself within his hazel eyes, and for once, the loudness in my life ceased to exist. He allowed me to breathe a sigh of relief that was taken from me in my childhood. He allowed me to be me, and cared for me in that.

My jumbled-up life was brought to a halt, finally.

He finally found me.

And, for once, I felt needed.

Scarlett

Hey Diary,

Was I being too overdramatic?

Sorry, haha.

It just didn't feel real to me at the time, but a hug is a hug. Obviously, I like the guy, but I will die on that hill that this hug meant something to me.

Maybe it was a hug that I never got from mom.

Or Monica.

Or Dad.

Something that I really shouldn't need to ask for, you know?

I just needed that support, and for once, I got it.

Scarlett

Hey Diary,

I think everything is finally the way it should be. Me and Leo are doing good, I think. That deserves an entry of its own, but regardless, everything is good.

Justin and Violet are dating now, which is cute. I never really expected it to be honest, but I'm not really that surprised. Jason still talks to me, thankfully. I really did mean it when I said I want our friendship to stick. He's a really good guy, and I know he'll find his own person.

I know Monica isn't necessarily happy with me about the whole Leo thing, I get it. We still talk sometimes, and we always smile when we see each other. I love that girl, really. I hope we can talk more like we used to.

Our school is holding a fair soon, and I want to ask Leo to go with me.

Scarlett

if only you were mine
may i find your
fingers grazing mine
finding their home
within my hand.

if only you were mine
with your smile
lighting your way into my heart
and your lips
wandering onto mine.

if only you were mine
id have proof
that a life without you
is a life not worth
living.

should you be mine,
my love will reach so far
my notes will stay in your pocket
my lipstick on your cheek
and my fingers grazing yours,
finding their way
to their home
within your hand.

scarlett

Hey Diary,

How was that one?

As you can see, it's pretty much inspired by him. I can't get him out of my head. All my thoughts are plagued with him. We hang out every single day at school. I spend all my free time during lunch with him. We do everything together. I've been texting Monica, and it seems pretty normal, so I can't imagine anything is wrong between us. I hang with Justin, Jason, and Violet outside of school, so it's not like I left them behind.

I can't imagine this year could've had a better start. Everything is going perfectly.

Scarlett

"scarlett, can we talk?"
5:01 pm

> "Yes, what's up?"
> 5:22 pm

"Well uh"
5:23 pm

"It's about Leo"
5:26 pm

> "Okay go for it"
> "Did he do anything?"
> 5:35 pm

"No its not that"
"It's just"
5:37 pm

> "Yes??"
> 5:51 pm

"Do you really like Leo?"
5:55 pm

> "Yes monica, I really like Leo"
> 6:05 pm

> "Why do you keep asking?"
> 6:08 pm

"Am I bothering you by asking?"
6:09 pm

"No, but you know I won't get upset if you
like him. I just felt like I've never really
gotten your support with it, that's all."
6:25 pm

"Oh"
"I see"
"I do support you scarlett"
6:26 pm

"That's all I've wanted to hear from you"
"I've never gotten that, you realize?"
6:30 pm

"no yeah i get it"
"can i please just ask one more question"
6:31 pm

"Sure"
6:55 pm

"just give me a second to figure out how to
ask"
6:56 pm

"Take your time."
7:01 pm

"do you like him, or do you like the idea of him?"
7:45 pm

"Dude, Monica"
8:12 pm

"no im not tryna be unsupportive"
"just"
"hear me out"
8:14 pm

"as long as i can remember, you've liked leo. hes always been just a footstep too far, and you finally have him. youve been chasing him your whole life, scarlett. are you in love with him, or are you in love with the chase?"
8:19 pm

"Read the first sentence of that text. There's your answer"
8:33 pm

"alrighty"
8:35 pm

Hey Diary,

I don't know what the deal with Monica is. She claims to support me, but doesn't want what's best for me?

Whatever.

I see Monica around and she still seems to be friendly with me, which I can't be mad about. She's a good friend, this is just our one disagreement.

On another note, I decided to ask Leo if he wanted to go to the school fair. He said yes!! I couldn't go last year so I'm so excited to go now! We sit right next to each other in class, and he grazes my thigh with his hand. It's kinda hot haha. I don't know if he does this on purpose, but I do NOT mind.

Scarlett

Hey diary,

The school fair is tomorrow, and I genuinely cannot wait for it. He is making me feel so excited. I want to kiss him, but I think it's too soon.

I know Monica is going too, but she's going with some other class friends. I don't know if I'll see her, but I'll say hi. I think everyone is going too, I know Justin, Violet, and Jason are going together.

I want the night to just be me and him, though. I think it's much needed.

Hopefully it goes well!

Scarlett

Oh.

Hey Diary,

I have never been more upset at Leo.

At the fair, he was with some friends that he didn't like, so he asked me to come and get him. Then, once I got him, we walked all throughout the fair. He held my hand for fucks sake. Apparently, he invited another girl from another high school, and he went with her.

He left me, for her. After all we've been through.

I told Monica, and she was not happy about it at all.

Scarlett

"I can't believe he would do something like that to you."
10:12 am

"I know, me too :("
10:15 am

"How do you feel Scarlett?"
10:16 am

"Betrayed honestly."
"I never expected him to do something like that."
"I thought we were doing so good too"
10:25 am

"Maybe it's for the best?"
10:26 am

"Yeah, maybe."
10:30 am

"Do you still want to talk to him?"
10:31 am

"I don't know. I want to see his side of the story"
"I don't want to throw away everything we had"
10:35 am

"Scarlett"
"How much did you really have with him?"
10:36 am

"I don't know. I might be overreacting."
"I've never felt anything like I've felt for
Leo, and you know that."
"I need to at least give it a try."
10:42 am

"well"
"as long as you're happy."
10:44 am

"I'll let you know if anything happens"
10:45 am

"you do that."
10:46 am

Hey Diary,

He apologized to me, and he didn't mean to toss me to the side.

Monica doesn't smile at me anymore.

I really don't know what's up with her these days. Leo always seems to be the common theme.

A part of me wishes we were 7 again. Walking to the corner store. Having fun in the school playground. A part of me wishes we weren't strangers anymore.

I'll always have love for her, and I'll always love her.

Maybe this is just how high school goes.

Scarlett

Hey Diary,

Happy birthday to me. Sweet 16.

I decided not to have a big party like other people at school. I hung out with Justin, Violet, and Jason. My mom went out with some friends, I think.

I also didn't celebrate on my actual bday, you know, since it's Christmas and all. I hung out with them after the New Years.

Justin got me a joint. Thanks Justin.

Jason awkwardly tried to kiss me, which I dismissed as a weird hug. Thanks Jason?

Violet got me a big basket full of things I like, which was honestly a really nice gesture. She also got me a joint. Thanks Violet.

Leo gave me a happy birthday text. That's it.

Scarlett

Hey Diary,

I think Leo is really starting to like me.
Thank God, it would've been pretty
awkward explaining that one to Monica.

I also think I finally found my crowd.
Justin, Jason, and Violet are always around
me when I'm not with Leo. Again, Jason
can't be bothered to take a hint. Even Justin
and Violet tell him on the side to just quit.
He knows I like Leo.

Boys, am I right?

With that, I've been smoking with Justin and
Violet even more. Not Jason anymore, he
kinda ruins the rotation. He always gets
philosophical about liking me. It's not that
serious, Jason.

Anyways, I'm gonna be taking a break from
writing for a bit. I have a lot of assignments
piling up on me.

Scarlett

You are inconceivably evil.

- helios and his moon

Dear diary,

I lost myself after the incident.

It happened during the end of the school year. It was such a beautiful day, too. Partly cloudy, just how I like it. It was in public.

Jason didn't even care that we were in public.

I don't know how I can go past this.

I didn't know how I could've survived it. I still don't. I've only told Justin and Violet, and they were just as mortified.

I think they told the school, or police, or both. He doesn't go to school with us anymore.

I wear baggy clothes to hide my body now.

Leo doesn't even know, and I don't plan on telling him.

S.D.

Dear Diary,

I've been skipping class a lot. I can't be around too many people before I get anxious. The school tells my mom, but she doesn't even care at this point. She's waiting on me to go to college to kick me to the curb.

Leo is the only one that I want there for me. Yes, Justin and Violet are there for me too, and I am super happy about that, but I want Leo to be there for me too.

I don't think he is.

He knows something is wrong, but he tends to avoid me when things are wrong. I want to be with him, and he wants to be with me. We have discussed that, but we both just need to work our own things out first.

S.D.

Dear Diary,

I've started to see a therapist.

She specializes in that kind of stuff for minors. She constantly reminds me that it is not my fault, but I can't help but feel that it is. I think I led him on, and it turned into this.

Regardless, he's gone. I won't have to see him again.

Leo and I hold hands through school, and he is making me feel safer than before. I think he is really serious about me and him now. I still need time, but he is making it a lot easier to trust again.

S.D.

Dear Diary,

I smoke weed a lot now. I know I shouldn't, but it takes the edge off. Sometimes it's with Justin and Violet, but most times it's alone.

Also, it was my birthday yesterday. This one was special, because it is the last birthday before I'm officially an adult. Sounds crazy, I know.

Mom went out and got drunk again. Didn't even celebrate Christmas this year. What a family dynamic, right?

My therapist says I have a fear of abandonment, which I kind of found hilarious. I've been abandoned my entire life. First, my dad, then, my mom.

I don't fear abandonment,

I fear what happens after.

S.D.

Dear Diary,

I read through my old diary as a little kid, and I found it so cute. A lot of it is still kind of relevant.

I still want to be a writer.

I believe writing is one of the most beautiful things a human can do. Writing is one of the only ways you can get 100% of emotions out. It's paper, it can't judge you.

Leaving something behind in life is my ultimate goal. I want to write until I cannot write anymore and leave my message behind. I want to reach millions and show people what I can bring to the world.

And, Leo will be right beside me.

Me and Leo are dating now, officially.

S.D.

Dear Diary,

I find myself to be at Leo's house more than my own. I don't have much of a support system at home anyways. At least his parents like me.

On a separate note, I don't see Monica as much as I used to. I still see her from time to time, but she got a lot more distant. We don't really text anymore other than asking each other for notes. We have a class together, by the way.

I just want to grow up already. I want to leave this place and leave these people. I want me and Leo to run away into a little cottage in Italy.

I want to not care about anyone.

S.D.

not once did i think
you were meant for me
i believed that
you, surely,
were meant for greater things.

you believed in me
you showed me what
undying acceptance feels like
and what past lives do
when they meet again.

you guided me along
slowly, gently
into a life worth living.

tomorrow, we'll be better

and always,

our love will show

in this life,

and the next

S.D.

Dear Diary,

I became the president of poetry club!

While that sounds like the lamest thing in the world, it means a lot to me.

It means people rely on my writing. People don't mind what I have to say, but listen when I must write. My essays always get 100%. My poems get published by the school. And, I gotta say, my birthday texts are always the best.

Leo said he was really proud of me, and that made me happy.

Sometimes, all I need to know is someone out there is proud of me. Sometimes, all I need to know is if someone is listening.

S.D.

Dear Diary,

It is the last of my junior year. It's an important date for me, because it marks the last day before I'm a senior. And, it's been a year since the incident.

I haven't learned to accept it, rather, I've learned to live with it.

Leo has been by my side this entire time, and I can't help but be so happy he's mine. Watching him grow into the man he is today has been the most rewarding part of my life.

I love Leo, and that is the beginning and end of everything. He has shown me what it is like to grow alongside someone, and he has shown me what it's like to truly accept someone.

I, wholly, accept him.

S.D.

Dear Diary,

Leo got me a promise ring today.

I didn't know what to say. I burst into tears at the sight of it. I immediately thought that we were too young to get married, then I didn't care, then he told me it was only a promise ring.

Hey, I'll take it.

I promised to love him forever, and that I will do.

He's done so much for me; it is only fair that I can do the same for him.

Instinctively, I went to text Monica.

I didn't. Sometimes, you just need to move on.

S.D.

Dear Diary,

It is the first day of senior year. Yikes.

I'm taking more writing electives so it can look good for college applications. It's also crazy that I have to worry about college now.

I see Monica a lot more now. I don't know why, it's not like she actively goes out of her way anymore to interact with me.

She looks at me. Sometimes twice.

I think she misses our friendship, and I do too. But college is around the corner, and we can't begin to act like we'll have a healthy enough relationship for college.

Regardless, I'm excited for this year. It'll finally be the end of high school.

S.D.

Dear Diary,

I can't help but smoke weed pretty much every day.

Well, not every day. Probably 4-5 times a week. My mom sends me money, which I guess is her way of saying she loves me. I don't know if she knows that's what I use her money for, and I don't think she cares anyway.

Leo cares, though.

He knows I smoked this whole time, but he's noticed that I've upped the pace.

I feel a lot better when I smoke, so I guess he just has to accept it. I've invited him to smoke with me multiple times, but I guess he just doesn't want to.

S.D

Dear Diary,

I tried shrooms today for the first time.

Holy shit.

I did not know that would last the entire day. I just wanted to take the edge off in the beginning of the school day.

I didn't know I'd be drooling with one eye open during my fictional writing class.

Leo wasn't too happy with me.

Justin was impressed.

Fuck yeah,

Thanks Justin,

                                        S.D.

Dear Diary,

I just sent in my applications for colleges.
I've never been more nervous while clicking
a "confirm" button.

I applied to a bunch of in-state schools to up
the chance of going with Leo. I applied to
the same schools as Leo, and we both have
around the same grades, so we should have
the same chances.

Justin and Violet also applied to the same
schools as each other, which was sweet.

I didn't think senior year would go by this
fast. I'm just wondering what it'll feel like
after the acceptance letters come back.

Anyways,

Hopefully I get into college at least, haha.

S.D.

5 years left.

Dear diary,

I'm 18 now.

Wow.

I don't feel any different, but I'm seen
differently by society now.

It really is hard to believe that I'm an adult.
It feels like yesterday that I was going to the
store after school with Monica and my mom.
It feels like yesterday that Monica was
giving me shit for Leo, and rightfully so, he
was not that good of a guy in the beginning
of our life together.

I feel like I have more responsibilities. More
obligations. I feel like now I am meant to
have a purpose in life.

A purpose, that I will hold up to the world.

S.D.

Dear Diary,

It's my last first day of school. My last
semester at this high school. Thank God.

College acceptance letters are coming soon,
which I cannot wait for. I am praying me
and Leo get into at least one school together,
that is all I need.

I need to leave this place. I want my home to
become a vacation. I want this city to feel
new. I want to leave and come back to the
feeling of uncertainty that I find in this city.

There are too many people in this city.

Too many people I cannot be around.

I owe a lot to this city, though. I found Leo.
I found a support group. And, I found
myself

S.D.

sometimes i look up at the stars
and wonder our place
within them.

i wonder
if the stars gaze back at us
with the same questions about us
as we have of them.

are shooting stars
leaving behind a trail
for us to gaze upon in wonder
or are they chasing after something
burning themselves up
in the meantime?

S.D.

Dear Diary,

I have no words. College acceptances came back today, and me and Leo got into the same schools!!! I am shaking as I'm writing this.

Instinctively, I went to text Monica, but that's a thing of the past now. Me and him were so ecstatic. I can't help but think of our future together now.

This means another 4 years together, at least. At the end of that, we'll be together for about 6 years.

I truly think I found the one for me for the rest of my life.

I got a pretty hefty scholarship to the school I'm accepting. My mom has no problem paying the rest, plus housing. She just wants me out of there.

So do I.

S.D.

Dear Diary,

I cannot bring myself to go to all of my classes in a day. Senioritis is real. I already got into college, what is the point in going to class?

Justin and Violet feel the same way, because we all ditch school to go to the park.

Yes, we smoke. Sounds like a typical high school delinquent thing to do, but I cannot be judged.

Yearbooks are starting to sell. Break-ups are happening. School is coming to an end.

It's hard to put a feeling like this on paper, which is the first time it's happened to me.

S.D.

Dear Diary,

I just got back from graduation. Walking across that stage, looking onto hundreds of students and parents made me emotional. I don't know what it is either. I always wanted to leave this place, so I don't know why it was so hard to finally do it. Watching people cry while hugging each other really did it for me. I cried while hugging Justin and Violet. They stuck with me throughout the entirety of high school, and we're going our separate ways. I guess this is how life goes, and how it's meant to be. Me and Monica made eye contact. I could tell she was wanting to come up to me, and something told her not to. I hugged and kissed Leo, and we knew it was the start of a new chapter for us. Us being together has been the highlight of my time here, and it'll only get better.

I'll miss everyone I met, but it's time to hit the real world.

S.D.

Dear Diary,

This summer has been a busy one. Getting everything ready to move into college has been super stressful. It's happening though, I'm moving in about a week.

Me and Leo are not in the same dorm hall, which is kind of annoying, but at least we're in the same school. That's all that matters. I'm happy I'm with him regardless.

No word from Monica this whole summer. I felt like she had something to tell me, but it's whatever at this point. I'm sure somewhere down the line, we'll make contact again.

I hope we do, I miss her.

S.D.

Dear Diary,

College is way scarier than high school. Everything feels so real. This is real life now. Everyone is being treated like adults, and it's because we ARE. I have to walk 20 minutes to go from my writing class to my math class and it's extremely annoying. I want to get a bike or a scooter, but I think that's kind of embarrassing haha.

I don't see Leo as much as I thought I would. I mean, we hang out every day, but I thought I'd see him physically on campus. I guess it's just too big.

No call from mom, either.

I don't know how often, if at all, I'll go home. I have a home here.

S.D.

Dear Diary,

College tests are no joke. I failed my first exam, and so did 99% of students in that class. At least, I'd like to think so. I also can't help but keep smoking. It really just takes the edge off, and at this point I do it every day.

I recognize it's not the best thing for me, but I do it anyways. Seems like I have that history in my life, right?

Anyways, I gotta get that grade up. I can't get kicked out my first semester. I genuinely don't know where I'd go from here.

I want to start joining organizations too, I want to feel like I really do belong with other people here.

S.D.

Dear Diary,

They had a club rush at school, and every organization was out. It was crazy seeing just how many more clubs they have in college than in high school. I joined the poetry club once again, are you surprised?

Also, I think I might be interested in sororities. I know they have a stigma against them, but they seemed really nice here. I don't think I have anything to worry about, I'll just check it out.

Anyways, I made a friend today. His name is Joshua. He's in my writing class, and he really reminds me of Justin. I felt really comfortable with him, and I think that's why.

It makes me happy that I'm making friends in college. I don't make friends easily, so this is a big step up for me.

S.D.

Dear Diary,

Sorority rush started today!

It was interesting. It felt very competitive, repetitive, and a little cult-like. I guess that comes with every Greek organization, I suppose. It was weird at times, but I feel like I really connected with this one organization. One of the sisters is in my chemistry class, and she actually recognized me. She really made me feel comfortable.

I'm trying to keep my options open, but it's a little hard to. Everything feels so surface level, but this organization really resonated with me.

Leo is also going through with fraternity rush, which is a whole process in itself, but we're both super excited to go through with it regardless.

S.D.

Dear Diary,

These girls really seem to like me. They always say hi to me, and even hang out with me! The girl who recognized me in chemistry sits next to me now. She told me she wants me in the organization, which just made me so happy.

All I want is to feel like I belong. I want to belong in every single aspect. Leo makes me feel like I belong, but I want more.

I love what Leo does for me, don't get me wrong, but I need a group of people to surround myself with.

Speaking of Leo, he's a cute little pledge now. He has to wear his polo and shorts every day now. Sometimes, if someone says his name, he starts doing pushups. It's funny, really.

S.D.

Dear Diary,

I guess I don't belong. They didn't invite me
to join their sorority. It's so annoying too,
because now that girl from chemistry isn't
talking to me. It was an overnight switch
from loving me to acting like I don't exist.
It's like they never really cared about me
after all.

Josh saw this and was really annoyed about
it. He saw how serious I was about it, and
how much it mattered to me.

Leo saw it too, and now he refuses to talk to
that sorority. Thanks Leo.

It just irritates me. I thought I belonged.

S.D.

Dear Diary,

Once again, happy birthday to me. Big 19.

I didn't go home for Christmas, but Leo did. My mom didn't even call me. She didn't even care that I didn't come back. She still pays for my college, so I know she recognizes my existence, but that is the extent of our relationship. Nothing but money.

I've also been coughing up a storm. I don't know if it's because of the weather, or what it could possibly be. Sometimes specks of blood come up, which scares me.

Once the holidays pass, I'll get it checked out. I'm not too worried, it doesn't happen very often.

See you again soon, Diary.

S.D.

There is no part of my life that could've prepared me for this.

Dear Diary,

I don't really know how to start this entry.
It's been a while since my last entry because
I just couldn't find the words to explain how
I feel.

I went to the doctor in the beginning of
January. I told him about a persistent cough,
and he decided to listen to my lungs. He was
a bit concerned, so he ended up running a
few tests.

To cut the bullshit, it came back.
It's manifesting as lung cancer now.

I don't want to treat it.

I've spent enough of my life worrying,
apologizing, and regretting. I want to live. I
want to live as much as I can in the time I
have left. I want to spend my remaining time
on Earth with the people that I love. I want
to experience the rest of my life with Leo.

S.D.

Dear Diary,

The coughing is definitely irritating, but nothing insane. It's a lot more frequent, but that's it.

Leo isn't taking the news very well. He couldn't stop crying for weeks. I can't blame him; I was doing the same. I'm not quitting smoking, either. I'm gonna go out doing what I love, haha. I want to write as many meaningful pieces as I can before I pass. I need to leave my mark on this world, whether it be through 20 people or 2 million people.

I can't help but think to myself that I'm being selfish. Am I? I feel like I can't find any good reasons to keep going.

I wish I could, but I can't.

S.D.

Dear Diary,

I told my mom. It was the first time I talked
to her in about a year. She didn't take it well
either, but I don't see her coming here to
spend time with me. This is exactly what
I'm talking about- I don't need to ask for
any more help. I think my life was made this
way. I think God made my life this difficult
and short because I was meant to make the
most of it. I was meant to spread a message
to people. I was meant to love, and that I
did.

I wrote, and I wrote. No matter how
important people find my words to be,
they'll always stay in this world. I want to
stay in this world with Leo, even far after I
am physically gone. I'll haunt his ass if
that's what it takes.

I'll watch over him, judge his every move,
and make sure he knows I'm there.

S.D.

Dear Diary,

It's getting pretty bad. I take a lot of time in between entries now because I go out a lot more than I used to. Leo got a second job to help pay for the stuff we do together. We're supposed to go on a cruise in a few months, which I'm really excited for.

I don't go to classes anymore, which I don't really mind. I don't know why I need to take more writing classes, since I am quite literally writing right now.

Leo is more depressed than he's ever been. I know he tries to put up a front with me to make me comfortable, but I see right through it.

Joshua is upset too. News spreads, I guess. He was crying to me about it, but I told him not to worry about me. It's not the end of the world, I'll come back and find them.

S.D.

Dear Diary,

In my last visit with the physician, he told me it is spreading. It spread to my thyroid, esophagus, and liver. He gave me one year left.

It takes a lot out of me to do daily tasks. It's hard to get up in the morning, mentally and physically. My cough has way more blood than it usually did, and my voice is a lot raspier than it once was.

If I lose my voice, then so be it. My entire life, I never really had one. I succumbed to addiction, peer pressure, and hate. I never spoke against it, nor did I feel like I could.

What I have for myself are my words. My hands, fingers, and palms. I have my mind. I can write the words of a dying woman. I can write the words of a loving man. I can write the words of a broken life, lived by the both of them.

S.D.

Dear Diary,

I'm so weak. My mind is weak. I cannot write like I used to. I try, but I can't seem to pinpoint certain emotions anymore.

Leo seems to be sad with me, and I feel terrible for him. I regret not getting help. I wish I listened to the doctor. I wish I never started smoking. I wish I listened to Leo.

Leo begged on his knees to have me get help, and I did nothing but laugh at him.

I'm on my deathbed, and my memories of Leo are laughing at him while I knew I was a dead woman. My last thing I did as a healthy person, was take away the only part of myself he loved. He loved me, and I took that away from him.

I wish I never did this; I wish I got help.

S.D.

Dear Diary,

I have 1 month left. I officially cannot
speak. My esophagus is riddled with cancer.
I have cancer everywhere in my body now, I
lost count how many dots popped up in that
picture. I'm living in the hospital for the rest
of my time being.

I had a lot of visitors in the beginning. Justin
and Violet came and cried. A lot. They
never thought my life would be this way,
and neither did I. Monica came to me and
gave me a letter, and told me to open at my
discretion. That's all she said. Leo stays
with me every day. I love that man, I wish
we could've experienced more together.

My life at this point is summed up in wishes.
I wish I did more. I wish I wrote more. I
wish I cared and loved myself more.

I also wish I belonged, I wish I was loved,
and I wish I talked to Monica more.

I didn't do any of that.

S.D.

The following is a voice transcript from Leo towards Scarlett.

Note Scarlett's inability to verbally reply.

"Scarlett, I can't sit around and watch you die. Don't reach for that notebook right now, just let me speak. Our entire life, I loved you. From the moment I saw you as little kids, I thought you were pretty. I thought you were the most loveable person in the world. I wanted to get to the bottom of you; I wanted to explore your mind."

...

"You were a mystery in my life Scarlett. I never really understood you. I didn't know why you constantly believed you were destined to be a martyr. You killed yourself, Scarlett."

...

"Yes, I know cancer isn't your fault, but you could've done something about it. I mean, FUCKING Christ Scarlett, you killed yourself. You don't fucking KNOW the damage this does to me. You don't have the ability to grasp what I feel watching my girlfriend die right in front of me. You were more alive in the beginning of this conversation for fucks sake."

...

"Scarlett, I will always love you. In this life and the next, I will love you. You will forever be my soulmate, but I've moved on. I moved on the moment you told me you wouldn't get help. I can't sit around loving someone who doesn't love themselves. I can't waste my life holding the hand of a dying girl. I can't give you any more shirts off my back. You can't rely on my anymore Scarlett. I have a life too."

...

"Jesus FUCK. I don't know what to do. I hope you go gentle into that good night, Miss Author. You would've laughed at that any other time, so why aren't you now? You're a shell of the person you once were. I hope the afterlife treats you as well as I did. I hope the afterlife treats you with kindness, fairness, and dignity. If you haunt me, I wish you could see the life that could have been. I wish we had more time together. I wish you had loved yourself more. Goodbye, Scarlett."

...

Scarlett Daniels passed away at 23 years old. She was surrounded by physicians and nurses that cared for her in the final year of her life. She did not have loved ones, nor did she have family accompaniment.

Scarlett spent the entirety of her life writing. She wrote and wrote until she couldn't anymore. She loved, and she was loved, despite all the times she felt otherwise. She did anything a teenager would've done and was judged harshly. No one deserves to die, including Scarlett. All Scarlett wanted was a voice. She wanted to be heard, and even that was taken away from her.

Scarlett reached out to me to be her voice, and I will be that voice for her. I will make sure she is known. I want her to experience the rest of her life, so I will publish this in hopes of carrying out her legacy, in order for her to find this in her next life. She'll know who to look for.

Monica gave Scarlett a letter, which remained unopened for the remainder of her life. The following section is the letter Monica gave to Scarlett.

Nicholas McDaniel

Dearest Scarlett,

My entire life, I was deeply in love with you. From the beginning of our lives together, I found myself needing to be around you. I knew, from the beginning, that you weren't into me. I was okay with that, because you were around me.

Then, you weren't. You were no longer around me. You had other friends, and that's okay, but I never moved on. I tried to like other girls, and I tried to like guys, but no one in life is Scarlett Daniels. When you told me about Leo, time and time again, I couldn't feel anything but jealousy. I felt as if I wasn't good enough for you, and I never said the right things.

I believed you loved me, Scarlett Daniels, but not in the way I loved you. I wanted exactly what was best for you, but you wanted what was best for other people. I suppose that's what led to this situation, because once I heard you were diagnosed again, I didn't feel surprised.

For the rest of my life, I'm going to think of what you've meant to me. I'm going to think of what could've been between you and me. And, I hope once your little diary is published for the world to see, you read it in your next life and find me. I have a few more words to say to you.

Scarlett Daniels, I will forever love you with the entirety of my heart. I am fully prepared to live alone for the rest of my life. You would be upset with me, but you can't really do anything about it, can you?

Scarlett Daniels, from the bottom of my heart, I wish you the best of luck. I wish you to see me in life, and I wish you to haunt me. I wish we had more time together.

Sincerely,

Monica Ramirez.

The following are the final words Justin had to say about Scarlett.

Violet declined an interview.

"Scarlett, I feel like I killed you. I introduced you to smoking and I feel like that killed you. I know you had cancer before, and that shit probably came back. I hope you forgive me up there, girl.

If you care, me and violet are getting married later this year. I wonder if you and Leo would have done the same. I believe we had a good life together, Scarlett. You were my best friend.

I love you, girl.

See you in the next life."

The following are the final words by Joshua.

"Scarlet, I'm so sorry. I wish me and you knew each other much sooner, and much longer. We didn't have a lot of time together in this crazy world. If you would've seen the boy I met this past month, you would've been proud. I love you so much girl, and I'm so sorry this happened to you.

I wish you the best of luck in the afterlife, and please visit me when you return. We have a lot to catch up on."

Leo declined an interview.

Upon multiple attempts to contact Scarlett's mom about an interview, a cease-and-desist letter was forwarded to my email.

No further attempt was made to contact her.

Monica accepted an interview offer.
The following is the entire transcript.

"Good afternoon, Monica."
"A little about me first, my name is Nicholas
McDaniel. I'm an author out of California
who is publishing Scarlett's story, as you
know-"

"Yeah, yeah, that's awesome!"

"-Yes, thank you! I am beyond honored that
Scarlett chose me to be her voice. With that,
I was really touched with your letter to
Scarlett. Would you like to touch upon
that?"

[Monica took a deep breath]
"Yeah, yeah, um. Obviously, I had feelings
for her. Since I could remember, I liked her.
It's crazy too, because, I never liked girls. I
liked Scarlett. She was the whole package,
ya'know?"

"No, definitely."

"Yeah. She was great. You know, I had a
sparkle of hope that she would've liked me
too, but I stopped getting that from her."

"What led you to believe that?"

"Believe what?"

"Like, you said you stopped getting the
feeling that she liked you. Why?"

"Oh. It wasn't like she liked me, you know?
My heart wanted something that wasn't
there. I made it obvious, too. I'd text her
back immediately every time we talked. I
stopped looking or hanging out with her
when she was with Leo. Normal relationship
stuff, you know?"

"Yeah, I get it. Sorry, have you been in a
relationship before?"

"Alright man, I haven't"

[Monica lit a cigarette]

"Do you smoke?"

"I'm okay, thanks."

"It's just..."

...

"Yes?"

"Maybe this'll take me to her eventually,
you know?"

...

"You're not over her, are you?"

"Don't think I ever will be."

"Every song reminds me of her, every drink I throw down reminds me of her. I close my eyes and there she is. It's a level of comfort to me I think."

"I think that's a beautiful thing, Monica."

"Why?"

"Well, you found your person."

"But what good does it do to me if she isn't around for me to experience her?"

"I've never met Scarlett in person. I don't know the type of person she is, I just have her writing here with me. In Scarlett's entire life, she hasn't had that voice. She barely even lived, you know?"

"Where are you going with this?"

"You let her live, Monica."

"What do you mean?"

"Your love for her transcended her. She is living through you. You allow her to experience life again. You allow her to see her words. She is you, and you are her."

"I never really saw it that way."

"That's why I'm the interviewer, huh."

[Monica chuckled]

"I guess you're right."

"So, I gotta ask. What do you think of Leo?"

"I think Leo killed Scarlett."

"Woah, easy there. What do you mean?"

"I think Leo drained the life out of Scarlett. I think she never deserved him. Everything I said about him to her wasn't out of jealousy. I mean, I was jealous, but that wasn't the main reason."

"That makes sense. I admire how much you protected her."

"I wish she did too."'

"How do you feel about the people who will
read this and see how you felt about her
from all perspectives?"

"I think, or at least I hope, it'll show people
how fucking good of a friend I am."

[We share a chuckle]

"No, really, what do you feel?"

"I don't know how it'll be. Honestly, I
probably won't even buy the book. I haven't
even read those entries. I don't wanna know,
it'll hurt me if I do. It's still too new for
me."

[Monica begins tearing up]

"You want a tissue?"

"No, it's okay, I got to get going anyway."

"Wait, before you go, one last question."

"Go for it."

"If you had one last thing to say to Scarlett,
what would it be?"

Monica did not speak for approximately 3 minutes

"I'd tell her I hate her. I'd tell her I hate her for how much she ignored me. For how much she threw me to the side. I'd cry and hit her until I am hysterical."

"Then, I'd tell her how much I love her. I'd tell her that I loved her glistening hazel eyes, her beautiful blonde hair, her soft skin. I'd tell her that I've been in love with her since the day I saw her. At times, fuck, I wanted to be her."

"Then, I'd say how much I'll miss her. I'm assuming she's dying anyway, so that's what I'm going off of. I'd say I'll miss her forever, and I'll never move on."

"You won't move on?"

"No,"

"What's the point of loving someone if you just move on?"

"Thank you, Monica."

"Thank you, Nicholas."

Monica was later found deceased in her home.

It was an apparent suicide.

The following note was found next to her.

me  scarlett

Scarlett's story serves as a reminder about life. Life will end, and life will move on. Life is the most brutal aspect about living, yet, life is full of love.

People are put on this earth to love. People are meant to take care of each other. People are never meant to move on, rather, people are meant to live.

Scarlett failed to live, and therefore, she failed to love. Scarlett wants her message to be extended to the world.

If you are reading this, take care of yourselves. Take care of other people. Love thy neighbor. Love thy brother and sister. Make use of the time you have. And, most of all, leave behind a message for the world.

This, I can say,

Scarlett did perfectly.

Nicholas McDaniel

Biography

My name is Nicholas McDaniel, and I am an author writing out of Downey, California. I wrote my first poetry book, *helios and his moon*, and reached the eyes of millions of people across 6 continents. *Letters to Another Life* hopes to encourage people to live unapologetically, and to encourage people to develop their voice. I love to write themes that explores people's greatest fears, and bring them into the light to be explored. I believe that writing is the truest window into the soul, and writing can provide a voice for anyone.

To all the Scarletts in the world, please let your voice be heard. Be loud.

To all the Monicas in the world, keep on loving. It's what makes the world whole.

To everyone else, start your legacy today.

Reach out!

Personal IG: heirofhelios
Writing IG: poetryfromnick
email: nmcdanielwriting@gmail.com